BUILDING
3D Digital Games

by Sarah Guthals, PhD

WILEY

BUILDING 3D DIGITAL GAMES

Published by: **John Wiley & Sons, Inc.,** 111 River Street, Hoboken, NJ 07030-5774, www.wiley.com

Copyright © 2018 by John Wiley & Sons, Inc., Hoboken, New Jersey

Media and software compilation copyright © 2018 by John Wiley & Sons, Inc. All rights reserved.

Alice 2.x © 2008-2017, Carnegie Mellon University. All rights reserved.

Published simultaneously in Canada

For general information on our other products and services, please contact our Customer Care Department within the U.S. at 877-762-2974, outside the U.S. at 317-572-3993, or fax 317-572-4002. For technical support, please visit www.wiley.com/techsupport.

Wiley publishes in a variety of print and electronic formats and by print-on-demand. Some material included with standard print versions of this book may not be included in e-books or in print-on-demand. If this book refers to media such as a CD or DVD that is not included in the version you purchased, you may download this material at http://booksupport.wiley.com. For more information about Wiley products, visit www.wiley.com.

Library of Congress Control Number: 2017953799

ISBN: 978-1-119-45347-5

ISBN: 978-1-119-45345-1 (ebk); ISBN: 978-1-119-45346-8 (ebk)

10 9 8 7 6 5 4 3 2 1

CONTENTS

PROJECT 4: CREATE AN ESCAPE ROOM MAZE

INTRODUCTION

SO YOU WANT TO MAKE YOUR VERY OWN 3D VIDEO GAME?
That is an awesome idea!

Making video games is *a lot* of fun, but it can be a lot of hard work, too. The video games that you play on your computer, game consoles, or even mobile devices were built by large teams of professional engineers over years! For example, the original *Legend of Zelda* took more than 100 people three years to make! What you will be building here won't be as polished as the games you play right now, but you can think of them as *prototype* games — models that you make to get your idea down and have your friends play. Then, when you have improved your idea and gained more experience, you can make it into a game that people can play around the world!

ABOUT ALICE

Alice is computer software that lets you make 3D video games faster and easier than with regular coding. It is a fun tool made by the researchers and engineers at Carnegie Melon University (CMU) in Pennsylvania. The brilliant people at CMU started creating Alice in 1999 and have been improving it for the past 20 years. Alice uses a block-based programming language that makes coding faster. You don't have to worry about making spelling mistakes or forgetting punctuation. Instead, you get to focus on the *logic* of your video game and making sure that it works.

Alice is software that you download, but you do not have to install it. You just download the file, double-click it, and use it! You might have to install Java to help it, though, because Alice uses Java to make your code run. Make sure you ask an adult for help and permission when you go to download Alice in Project 1.

ABOUT THIS BOOK

Building 3D Digital Games has four projects that guide you through how to create a storyline for your games and how to build some simple video games. In the process, you learn to use Alice so that you can build your own video games. In this book, you

» Find out how to write code in Alice

» Create a world for your game and add characters to it

» Make your characters move, talk, and perform actions

» Set up a game with players fighting zombies!

If you're reading this as an e-book, you can click or tap web addresses to visit websites mentioned in the book, like this: www.dummies.com.

This book has many steps with screen shots, and the highlighted text draws your attention to what to look for in the figure.

ABOUT YOU

Everybody has to start somewhere, right? I had to start writing this book by assuming that you're comfortable doing these things:

» **Typing on a computer and using a mouse**. You may know how to use a Windows system or a Mac; either one will do. This book shows examples on a Mac.

» **Following instructions**. Coding is very precise, which means that you have to do it exactly right. There are a lot of pieces to the puzzle when you are making a mobile app. You have to follow instructions carefully, and compare the pictures in the book to what you see on your own screen.

ABOUT THE ICONS

As you read through the projects in this book, you'll see a few icons. The icons point out different things:

Watch out! This icon comes with important information that may save you from trouble that professional coders sometimes have.

The Remember icon comes with ideas that you should keep in mind.

The Tip icon marks advice and shortcuts that can make coding easier.

PROJECT 1 GETTING ALICE AND MAKING A SIMPLE GAME

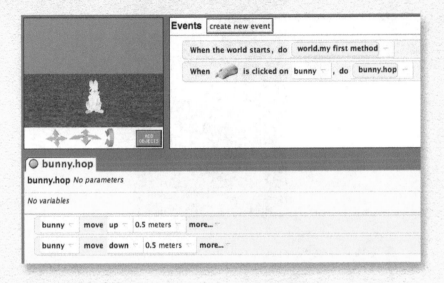

PLAYING VIDEO GAMES IS A TON OF FUN, BUT MAKING YOUR OWN IS INCREDIBLE! You get to create the characters, tell the story, and even code some Easter Eggs (fun secrets you put into your game that no one else knows about). In this project, you learn how to use the software called Alice, which will help you create your very first video game. You also learn the basics of coding. Alice is actually used in college to teach coding to college students, too!

DOWNLOAD AND START USING ALICE

To get started, you need to download and open Alice. Follow these steps to do that:

1 **Go to Alice.org. You should see a menu on the left side with a menu option called Get Alice. Click that.**

 Always ask permission from an adult before downloading or installing anything onto your computer.

2 **Scroll down until you see Alice 2. Click Get It.**

3 **Download the English Gallery Complete version of Alice 2 for your computer.**

Make sure you download the correct version for your computer. In this book, the example downloads the Mac version, but your computer might need the Windows or Linux version, which is fine. If you are using Windows, you will need to unzip the file by right-clicking and choosing Extract All. Then follow any instructions to extract the Alice files.

Alice 2

Alice 2 has a proven record as a great tool for learning logical and computational thinking skills and fundamental principles of programming. While it does not support the more advanced scaffolding of Alice 3 it remains a great first experience with the Alice environment and an option for a first step into the Alice world. There is world class curricular support that has been created over more than a decade of usage. The extensive gallery also include Garfield characters thanks to a generous partnership with Paws Inc. and supports the import of user created models.

Downloads

English Gallery Complete

Windows

Mac

Linux

You do not have to install Alice! It is just a file that you download (unzip it if you're on Windows). Then you can open it by double-clicking it. However, on some machines, downloading and unzipping might take a long time (more than ten minutes). If you are stuck, visit http://alice3.pbworks.com/w/page/58034183/Download%20Alice%202_3 for help on downloading on any computer.

4 **Double-click the Alice icon to open the software.**

After all the files have been extracted, you should see an Alice 2.4.app file on Mac and Alice 2.4.exe file on Windows. Double-click that file to run Alice.

Alice 2.4

You may get a Java Not Found error. If you do, you have to download and install the Java JDK from Oracle. The website to visit is http://www.oracle.com/technetwork/java/javase/downloads/jdk8-downloads-2133151.html.

Make sure that you get help from your adult and that you download the correct version for your computer.

5 **You should see a world chooser (a screen showing pictures of different types of worlds). Now you are ready to get coding!**

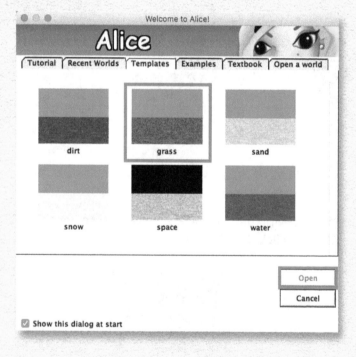

THE FIVE DIFFERENT ALICE PANES

Now that Alice is working on your computer, choose the Grass world. You should see the coding environment.

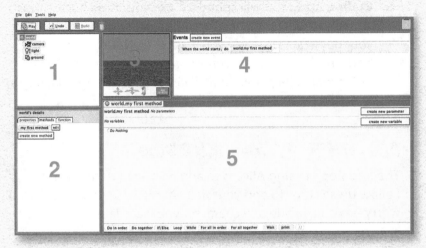

The coding environment has five main areas for you to understand. They are numbered in the figure and described here:

1 **Object:** In this area, you can find all the objects in your world. Every world starts with a camera, a light, and a ground, but you will add other objects to the world later.

2 **Object details:** Each object has details associated with it: properties, methods, and functions. Later in this book, you will learn about these different details because they will be the main part of coding!

3 **The world:** This is your scene in your world. You can use the arrows to move the camera around to see different parts of the world. You click Add Objects to add new objects. You see how to do this in the next section of this book.

4 **Events:** This is how you make games playable. Adding events to your game, like one called When an object is clicked, lets your players interact with your game.

5 **Coding area:** You will spend a lot of your time here. This is where you put all the instructions in the right order so that your game acts the way you want it to. Notice that at the bottom of this area are *control statements*, such as Do in order, which help you do really interesting things like repeat actions.

ADD OBJECTS TO YOUR ALICE WORLD

The first step in using Alice is to add an object to the world. Follow these steps to add your first character to your world. Don't worry — you can add any character you want later.

1 **Click Add Objects in the World area of Alice.**

2 Choose the Animals category.

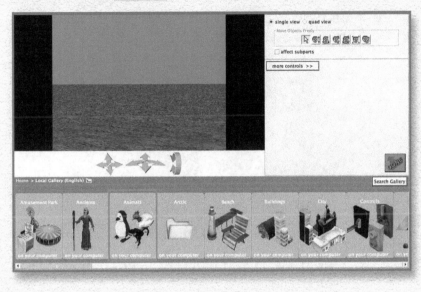

3 Add the bunny to your world. You can do this in two ways:

A **Click the bunny and then click Add instance to world.**

This will place the bunny in the center of the world, and then you can move it later.

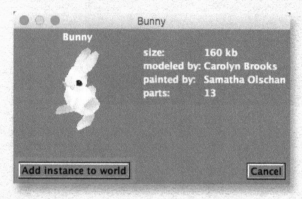

B **Click and drag the bunny into your world where you want it.**

This will place the bunny where you let go of it, and you can still move it later.

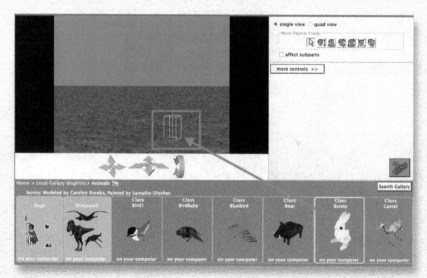

MAKE AN OBJECT MOVE

Now you can practice making your object (in this case, your bunny) move.

After you move the bunny, it is really hard to get it back exactly the way you want it. This can be frustrating if you move the bunny down a little and it goes underground. Be patient. If it's not going well, you can always delete the bunny by right-clicking it and then clicking Delete on the menu that appears. Then add a new bunny.

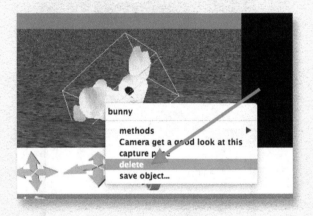

If your bunny is underground, or anywhere where you can't find it, you can delete the bunny by right-clicking the name of the bunny in the Object pane and choosing Delete. The Object pane is the first area in the "Five Different Alice Panes" section, earlier in this project.

1 **Click the bunny. A yellow cube should appear around the bunny. This cube means that you can move the bunny around.**

You can also click bunny in the Object pane to make the yellow cube appear around the bunny!

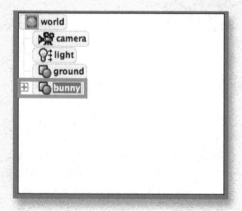

2 In the top right of the Add Object pane, you can see seven buttons that let you move the bunny in different ways. In order from left to right, click the buttons like this:

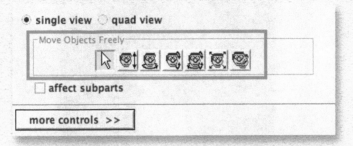

A First button: Move the bunny forward, backward, and side to side, but do not let the bunny move up and down.

B Second button: Move the bunny only up and down.

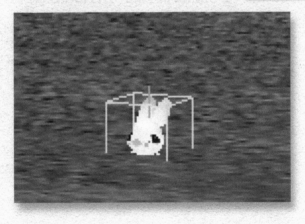

C **Third button: Spin the bunny around side to side, but do not move its location.**

D **Fourth button: Spin the bunny around forward and backward, but do not move its location.**

E Fifth button: Spin the bunny around side to side and forward and backward, but do not move its location.

F Sixth button: Make the bunny bigger and smaller.

G **Seventh button: Make a copy of the bunny so that you can have two!**

With the Make a Copy button, you can copy your bunny as many times as you want! You can keep making copies until you have 100 bunnies in your world if you want. Just be careful, because if you add too many bunnies, it will be hard to figure out which one you're coding for. Too many also might make the Alice software crash.

If you duplicate your bunny, you will see a second bunny object in your Object pane, too.

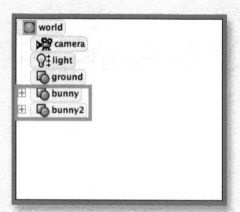

3 After you have placed your bunny where you want it, click **Done** in the lower-right corner. Now you will use code blocks to make your bunny the star of its very own movie!

Working with code blocks is how you write code in Alice.

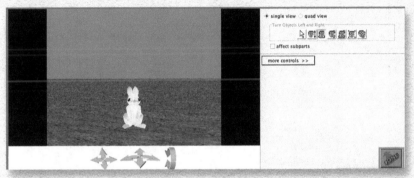

BE SURE TO SAVE YOUR WORK – OFTEN!

Alice does *not* automatically save your work, and sometimes the program crashes. That means that it shuts down on its own, and you could lose your work. Every 15 minutes, Alice will ask you if you want to save your program. You should *always* click Save right now. You should save even more often than 15 minutes, too, but at least every time Alice asks, make sure you save!

The first time you save your project, you will be prompted to name the project and choose a folder to save it to. If you ever want to save your project and the pop-up doesn't appear, you can choose File and then Save World. Be sure to do this before closing Alice!

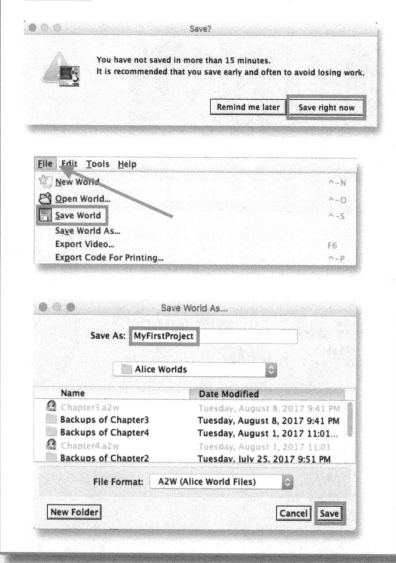

Anytime you want to start a new Alice project, make sure you have saved your project and then click File ⇨ New World, which will take you back to the same world chooser that you saw in the section "Download and Start Using Alice," earlier in this project. To open a world you have previously saved, click the Open a World tab in the world chooser to find your previous world and continue to make changes, or just to show your friends and family!

MAKE A SIMPLE MOVIE

Now that you have added an object, your Alice should look something like this. You probably moved your bunny around differently, and that's fine.

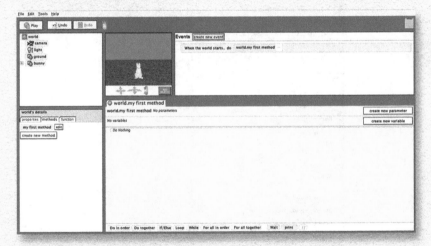

The first step to building a video game is to make objects move around in your world. Start by making the bunny hop:

1   Click the bunny.

You can either click the name of the bunny in the Object pane (upper left) or click the bunny in the world. Either way, the name in the Object pane should then appear highlighted and the yellow cube should be around the bunny. In the bunny's details on the bottom left, you should see methods for the bunny.

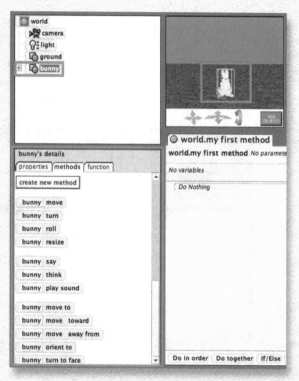

Alice has some code blocks already made for you, such as move. When you create a new method, you put together a set of code blocks and give that set a name. For example, you might create a method called dance that could have all the code for the dance moves for your bunny.

Methods are useful for splitting up code when it gets really long. They help you keep all the code organized. You will use more methods in later projects in this book.

2 **In the Object Details pane, you should see a code block in the Methods tab that says bunny move.**

3 **Drag the bunny move code block into your coding area, which is the pane to the right. When you drag it into the area that says Do nothing, a menu should appear.**

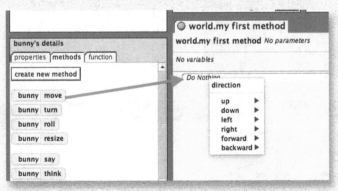

4 Hover over the arrow next to the up menu item and then click ½ (0.5) meters.

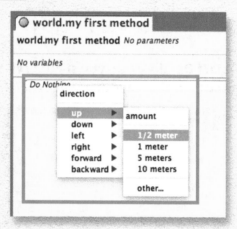

You should see one line of code in your world, the my first method tab. This line will execute when the world starts, because that is the event that is listed in the Events pane at the top.

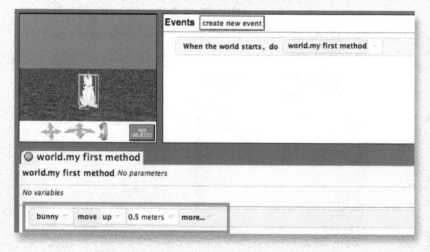

TEST YOUR MOVIE CODE

Now that you have some code written, you can test it!

Testing often is important! Coding can be a little tricky, and we all make mistakes. If you test your code often, you find your errors sooner, and fixing them will be easier. If you write all your code and test only at the end, finding the error might be harder.

1 **Click the green Play button at the top left of your screen and watch the bunny move up.**

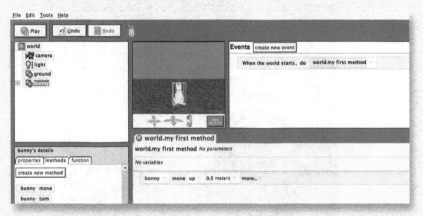

2 **Click Restart to replay the animation.**

When your movies and games get longer, you can speed them up using the speed controller (the slider in the top left under Speed) or click Pause to stop them. You can even click Take Picture to get a picture of what's happening. When you take the picture, Alice will store it on your computer and tell you where you can find it.

3 **When you're done playing your movie, click Stop.**

The window closes and and you return to the screen with the five panes.

CODE ANOTHER ACTION

So far, the bunny moves up, but it doesn't come back down! Add another bunny move code so that the bunny moves back down ½ (0.5) meters after it moves up. To do this, click the bunny to see the yellow cube. Drag the bunny move method to the coding area to the right. In the menu that appears, click the arrow next to down and choose ½ (0.5) meters.

Now you should have two lines of code blocks, on your my first method tab.

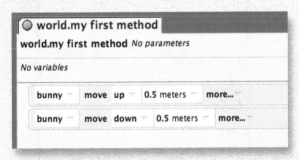

Be sure to click the Play button to test that your bunny does what it's supposed to do: hop!

MAKE A BUNNY HOP GAME

Instead of having your bunny hop right when you click the Play button, you can make your bunny hop whenever you click the bunny instead! This isn't the best game ever, but it does show you how to make methods and new events. You will use what you learn here in the next project to make a real game.

1 **Click your bunny in the Object pane and then click create new method in the bunny's details pane.**

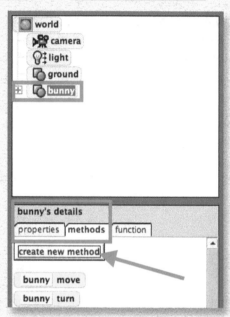

2 **In the New Method box that appears in the middle of your screen, type hop to name the method.**

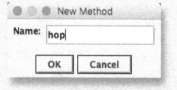

Your new method should show up in the Coding area on the lower right as another tab called bunny.hop. The tab with world.myfirstmethod will still be in the Coding area as well.

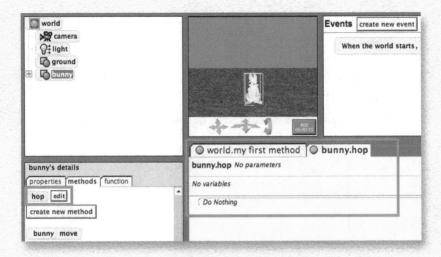

3 **Add the two code blocks, move up 0.5 and move down
0.5, to make your bunny hop in your new hop method.
These are the same two code blocks that you added to
world.myfirstmethod earlier in this project.**

*Methods are used to combine code blocks into logical
chunks. At first, you had the move up 0.5 and move
down 0.5 code blocks in world.myfirstmethod to have
all your code in one place. World.myfirstmethod is
called in the Events pane when the world starts.
You're now changing your code so that your new
method, bunny.hop, will be called when you click the
bunny. In later projects, you will create a lot of
methods that get called at different times.*

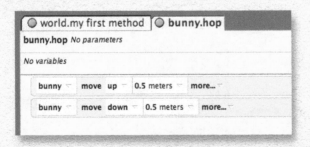

If you can't remember how to do this, go back to the section called "Make a Simple Movie."

4 **Remove the move up 0.5 and move down 0.5 code blocks from your my first method tab.**

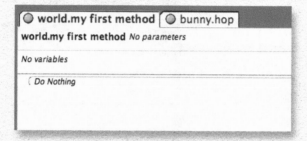

You can remove them in two ways:

A **Right-click each one on the right side (away from the words on the block) and click delete.**

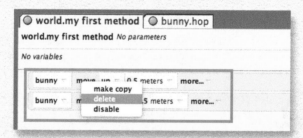

B **Click-and-drag the block to the trash can above the world pane.**

5 Go to the Events pane and click **create new event**. Then choose the **When the mouse is clicked on something** event type.

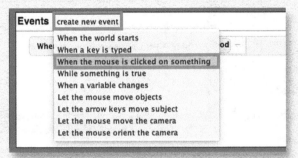

6 Change the object **anything** to **the entire bunny**.

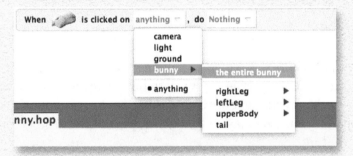

7 Change the method **Nothing** to **bunny.hop**.

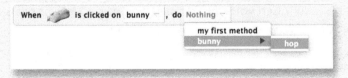

8 **Press Play and click your bunny.**

Every time you click the bunny, it should hop!

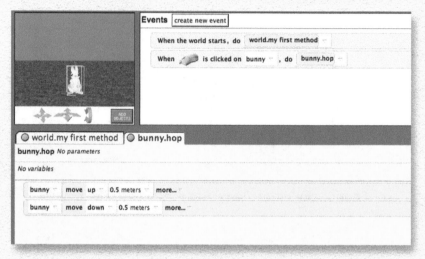

Congratulations! You made a simple movie in which a bunny hops! In the next project, you learn how to make an actual game, in which players can affect what is happening instead of just watching a movie play. In that game, your players can go on an adventure.

Even though this project is done, you should play around with Alice, adding more characters and trying other coding blocks. There is so much you can do, and this book covers only a small amount of it. So don't be afraid to explore!

PROJECT 2 ADVENTURE GAME – PART 1

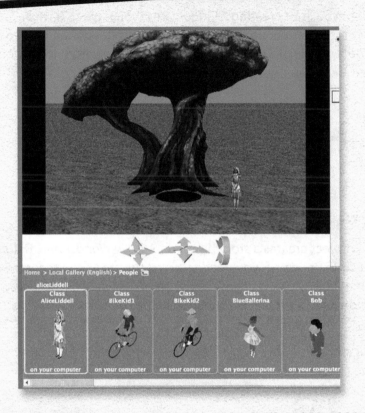

ARE YOU READY TO CREATE YOUR VERY OWN STORY-MODE VIDEO GAME? In this kind of game, a story is told, but the players get to choose where to go and how to react. For example, you can hide Easter Eggs in the game (little things that happen that players will discover, like a firework show or something). You can even put "cheats" in it so that if you press on the correct flower, you get to the end automatically. Get ready to make your favorite story come to life!

DESIGN YOUR FAVORITE STORY

Before you start creating a video game, you have to have a story for your game to follow. For this project, you can pick your favorite movie, book, game, or even short story from when you were a kid. You can make one up, too, if you want!

If you have trouble deciding what story to choose, just follow along with the story that this project uses. You can always make a second game later and use your own story.

OUTLINE YOUR GAME

This project creates a story based on *Alice in Wonderland*. Before you code the game, you need to break the story into scenes so that you know what your video game will look like. You also decide what your players should be able to do in different parts of your story world.

Your story probably won't have every single part of the story you have chosen, but that's okay! You can always add more to the game later.

STEPS TO CREATE YOUR OWN OUTLINE

To get started, follow these steps:

1 Choose your scenes.

For this project, choose up to three scenes in which something will happen. You do not want the world to get too big just yet, so it's best to start small.

2 Decide what happens in each scene.

Each scene should have some interactive part where players get to do something. Decide what that will be for each scene.

3 Design your AI (Artificial Intelligence).

In each scene, players get to interact with the world. Also, characters that are not controlled by humans, but instead are controlled by your code, will also do things. These characters are called *NPC*, for Non-Player Characters. The code that controls them is called *AI*, for Artificial Intelligence.

4 Choose an ending.

Decide how your game will end. Will characters have to collect things? If so, is that how they win or lose? What happens if they win, and what happens if they lose?

THE OUTLINE FOR THIS PROJECT'S EXAMPLE

Here is the outline for the *Alice in Wonderland* game created in this project. Note that Steps 2 and 3 have been mixed together, but both are still there.

1 Choose your scenes.

This project recreates two scenes in *Alice in Wonderland*: when Alice falls down the hole under the tree, and when the characters have a tea party.

2 Decide what happens at each scene/Design your AI.

A Scene 1 — Falling Down: First, a tree appears, and when Alice walks up to it, the screen turns black. Different household objects move from the bottom of the screen to the top of the screen to make it look like Alice is falling. After about 10 seconds, the screen lightens up again and Alice is at the tea party.

B Scene 2 — Tea Party: You see a long table with a bunch of snacks and drinks on it. Sitting at the table are the Mad Hatter, the Hare, and the Mouse.

3 **Choose an ending.**

In the tea party scene, the Mad Hatter, Hare, and Mouse all start singing "A very merry unbirthday" to the player!

When you create a game, you should spend some time outlining your game. It's okay to make the storyline in your video game shorter than the original story. This is the first version, and you can always add more later.

BUILD YOUR FIRST SCENE IN ALICE

Here comes the first part of actually building your game: building your scenes. In Alice, it can be tricky to get every item exactly where you want it. Don't worry about making it look perfect. Video games that you buy at the store have hundreds of people working on them for years before you ever get to play. You are going to make a game all by yourself, so it won't look perfect, but that's okay!

Before getting started, make sure you are working in a brand-new project. If you still have your project from Project 1 open in Alice, make sure you save it by clicking File ⇨ Save on the menu bar in the upper-left corner of the Alice software. Then create a new grass world, just as you did in the section "Download and Start Using Alice" from Project 1.

This first part of the project takes you through building the three scenes in the game based on scenes from *Alice in Wonderland*. You can follow along or make your own three scenes.

BUILD SCENE 1: THE TREE

Scene 1 for *Alice in Wonderland* is interesting because you will need a tree with a hole, but then you will also need to add code to allow Alice to move around the world. Follow these steps to make all these things happen:

1 **Click Add Objects.**

2 **Click the Nature category.**

3 **Find a tree that you like.**

4 **Add the tree to your world. To do this, drag the tree from the Nature category into the scene and release the mouse when the tree is where you want it.**

SET UP YOUR CAMERA

In Alice, you see the entire world through a camera. The controls for the camera are those large, gray arrows in the white area under the world. You can move the camera around to get a better look at different parts of the world, or different characters. As you will see later in this project, you can even attach the camera to a character so that your players can have the character's point of view!

You need to be able to move the camera around the world so that you can get different points of view and can change scenes.

Moving the camera can be tricky, so use this tip! When your camera is in an important position, such as when you can see the starting scene of your game, leave an object in the world exactly where the camera is. Then you can move the camera to other places in the world, but easily get the camera back to the original position.

Here are the steps to moving the camera:

1 Click the Shapes category.

2 Find the sphere.

3 Click Add instance to world to add the sphere to the world.

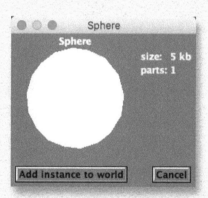

4 **Right-click the sphere in the Object Tree and click rename.**

5 **Rename the sphere to startLocation.**

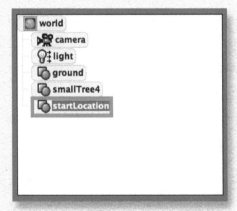

6 **Right-click the startLocation in the Object Tree and follow the menus that open: methods ⇨ startLocation. move to ⇨ camera.**

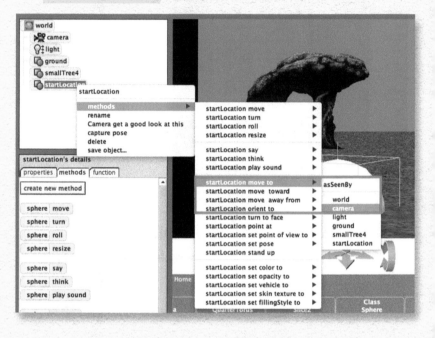

7 **Right-click the startLocation in the Object Tree again and follow the menus that open: methods ⇨ startLocation set point of view to ⇨ camera.**

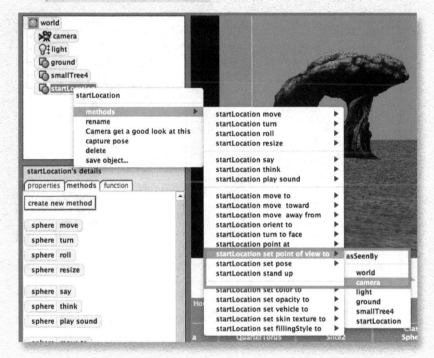

8 **Right-click the startLocation in the Object Tree and follow the menu: Methods ⇨ startLocation set opacity to ⇨ 0% Invisible.**

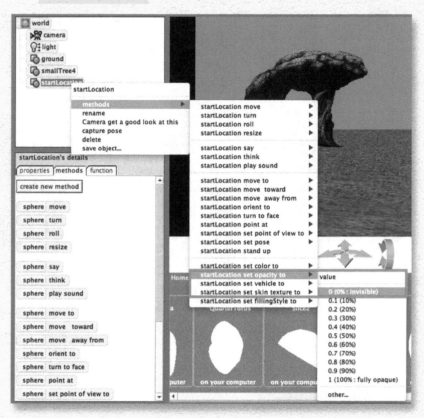

9 Using the arrows below the scene, move the camera to be closer to the tree.

10 Repeat Steps 1–8 with a second sphere, but name the second sphere treeLocation.

11 The Object pane should now have two locations that the camera can move between.

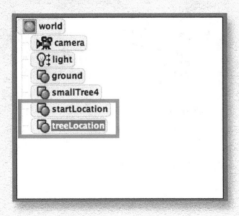

ADD ALICE AND THE HOLE

Now you can add the hole that Alice falls into, and add Alice herself!

1 **Add a circle to the world, right underneath the tree.**

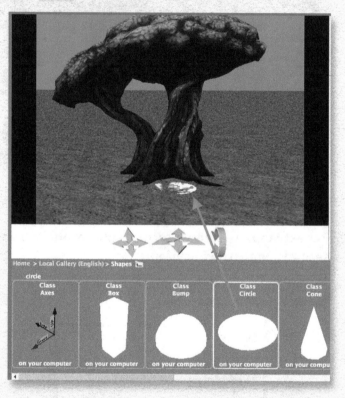

Click-and-drag the circle to the tree. As you drag the circle, a yellow box appears on the grass to show you where the circle will end up. Don't let go of the mouse until the circle is where you want it to be.

2 Right-click the circle in the Object Tree and follow the
menu: methods ⇨ circle set color to ⇨ black.

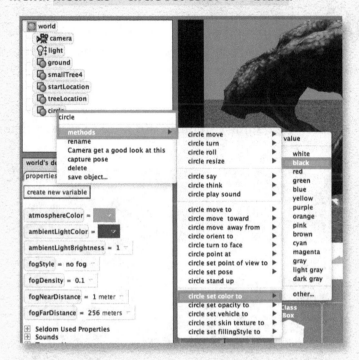

3 Click the Move Objects Up and Down option and move
the black circle up so that it looks like a hole in the
ground.

Sometimes when objects are very close to each other, moving a certain object can be hard. For example, when you try to move the circle up, you might accidentally move the ground up! Click the Undo button right next to the Play button above your Object pane if you need to undo your action and try again.

4 Under the People category, add Alice to the world, next to the tree.

5 **Click Done to go back to the coding area.**

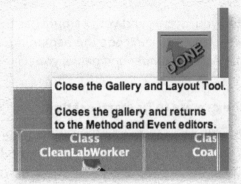

TWO WAYS TO CALL A METHOD

You have two ways to call a method (meaning, make an object perform an action). You can right-click an object in the Object Tree and select a method there. Or you can add a method as a coding block in the coding area. What's the difference between these two ways?

The difference is in when the action happens. If you right-click the object in the Object tree, as you do in Step 2 of the "Add Alice and the Hole" section, you are making that object do something *now* and *once*. If you add the block to the coding area instead, the action will happen only when certain other actions occur, like these:

» Someone presses the Play button.

» An event happens that you want your action to follow. This event might be when the world starts, or when someone clicks the object.

CODE SCENE 1

You've created your scene, and your camera has two locations to move between. Now you can code the beginning of Scene 1. To do this for the *Alice in Wonderland* game, you have to code the following steps:

1 Move the camera to its startLocation.

To do this, click the camera in the Object pane and find the camera move to code block under the Methods tab. Drag that code block into world.my first method. When you let go of the mouse, a menu appears. On this menu, choose the object that you want the camera to move to. In this step, you want the camera to move to the object called startLocation. You made this object in Step 5 in the "Set Up Your Camera" section.

2 Set the camera's point of view to the startLocation.

Do this just as you did in Step 1 in this section.

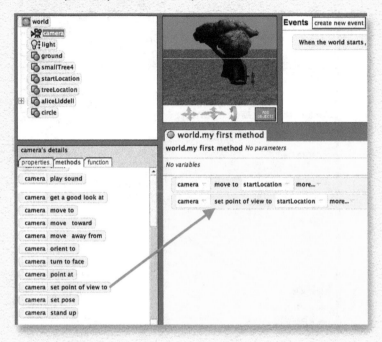

3 Have Alice introduce the game.

Make sure that you click the aliceLidell object in the Object pane before you drag the code blocks over. This makes Alice be the one talking. First, drag an aliceLidell.say block into your coding area and choose other for what she should say.

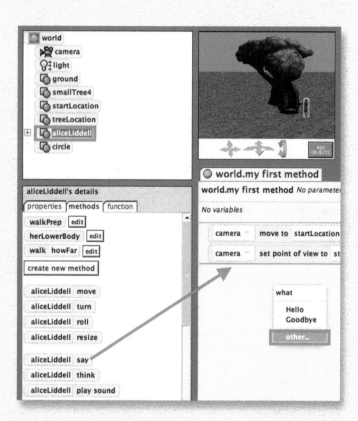

This will cause a text input box to appear in the center of your screen. Type in the message you want aliceLidell to say.

When you complete the aliceLidell.say block, your world. my first method should have three code blocks.

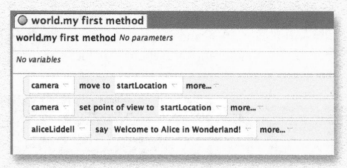

4 **Move the camera to the treeLocation and move set point of view to (the point of view of the camera) to the treeLocation.**

This is just like Step 1 and Step 2 in this section, except you should choose the object treeLocation instead of startLocation.

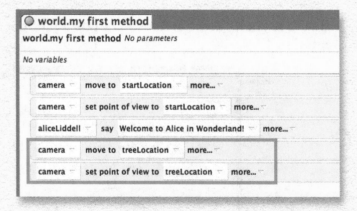

5 Add the turn to face code block to point the camera toward Alice.

To have the camera look at aliceLidell, make sure you choose the entire aliceLidell, and not just her head or feet, from the pop-up menu that appears when you place the turn to face code block.

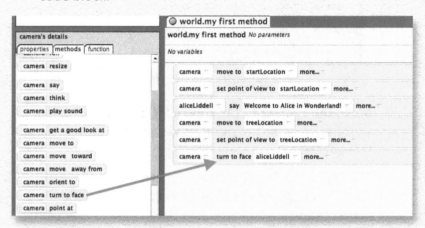

6 Add the say code block to have Alice talk about the rabbit.

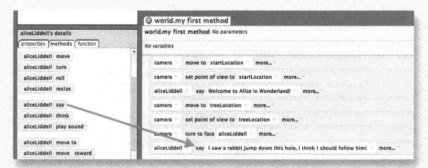

7 Hover on **move to** and follow the menu sequence to move the camera to the entire head (Alice's head).

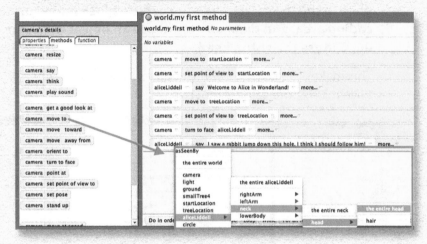

8 Set the **point of view** of the camera to Alice's head's point of view. When you drag the camera.set point of view to code block into your coding area, a pop-up will appear to allow you to choose a character. Choose aliceLidell, and instead of clicking entire aliceLidell, follow the pop-up menu to neck and then head to get the point of view to be only her head. Otherwise, the camera would be in her belly, which would make her seem very short!

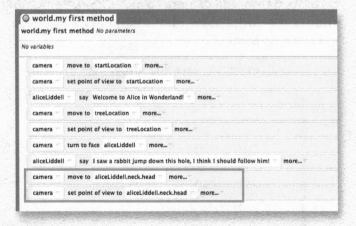

Find the camera's vehicle by clicking the **camera** in the Object pane. Then click the Properties tab in the Details pane in the lower left. Drag the **vehicle** block into your coding area, and the menu to choose an object will come up. Choose **the entire head.**

This makes the camera's vehicle Alice's head so that when Alice moves, the camera moves.

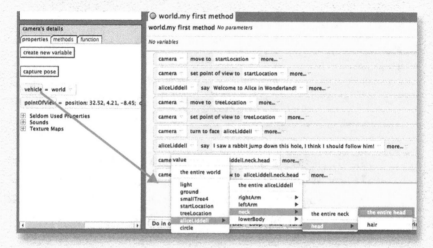

9 In the Events pane, click **create new event** and choose **Let the arrow keys move subject.** Then change the object to be moved from the camera to **aliceLidell.** Remember to choose **the entire aliceLidell** so that her arm doesn't just move on its own!

This adds an event to make the arrow keys move Alice.

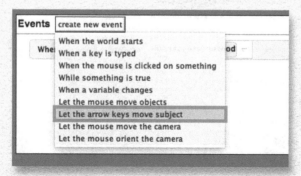

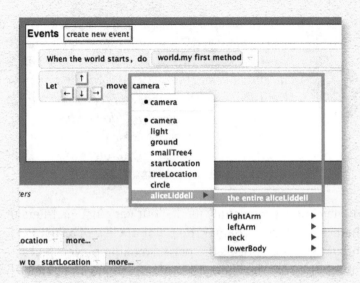

Now your code should look like the code in the following figure. When you click Play, you should see the camera move to the start position and then to the tree. Next, the camera goes inside Alice's head. Then you should be able to move Alice around with the arrow keys, and the camera should follow along.

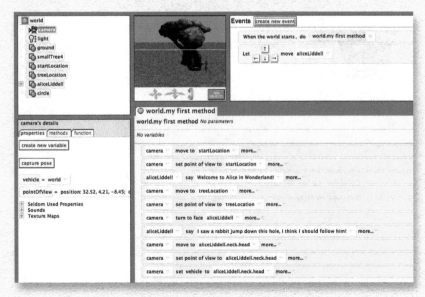

What if you have to take a break from coding? Or you finish and want to take a look at the code again later? Make sure to always click File ⇨ Save before you close Alice so that all your changes are saved. When you want to open Alice again, be sure to open the Alice software, just as you do in Project 1, "Download and Start Using Alice," Step 4. Then open a World tab and choose your project. (You won't have to choose a world this time.)

You have now successfully made your very first First-Person Character in a video game! The point of view of a First-Person Character is the same as the player, making players feel as though they *are* the character when they play the game. This first part of the *Alice in Wonderland* game isn't very fun yet because Alice just runs around a tree and can't even fall through the hole yet. In Project 3, Adventure Game — Part 2, you will create and code two more scenes: Alice falling down the rabbit hole and Alice finding the tea party.

Don't worry if things are getting confusing and you need help. You can find extra resources (videos and a forum to ask questions) at https://www.thewecan. zone/designing-3d-digital-games.

ARE YOU READY TO MAKE YOUR FIRST VIDEO GAME MORE EXCITING? In this project you will keep working on the same game you made in Project 2, but you will have Alice continue her adventure into Wonderland, falling down the rabbit hole and finding the tea party!

If you closed Alice already, make sure you open Alice, click Open a World in the world chooser, and click your Project 2 world. Then click Open. If Alice is already open, but you have a different Alice project open, you can do the same thing by clicking File ⇨ Open World in the menu bar at the top left.

PREPARE THE NEXT SCENE

In this section, you create a new scene. In the *Alice in Wonderland* game, you want to make Alice look like she is falling. You do that by making objects go up while Alice watches them.

First, you create the area where Alice will watch those objects. Follow these steps:

1 **Click Add Objects.**

2 **Use the arrows under the world to move the camera so that it points to an open area in your world.**

3 **Click the Shapes category and find a square. Click and drag a square to the world in front of your camera.**

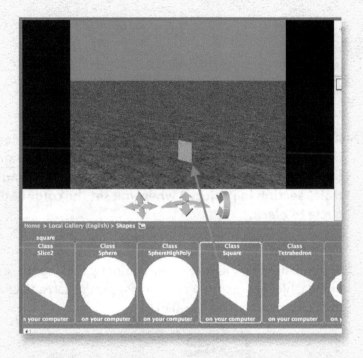

4 Use the object movement buttons to the right of the scene to move the square so that it is facing your camera and covers the entire area. You may have to use the arrows under your scene to point the camera up a bit so that you cannot see the grass anymore.

If you want to move or resize objects in your world, you can use the object movement buttons, just as you did in Step 3 in the section "Add Alice and the Hole," in Project 2. The resize button is the one with arrows pointing away from the man's head.

5 **Right-click the square in the Object pane. Then choose methods ⇨ square set color to ⇨ black. This is the same type of action you did in Step 2 in the "Add Alice and the Hole" section in Project 2 when you set the color of the circle to black.**

This changes the color of the square to black.

You can also change the square's color by clicking the square in the Object pane. Then click the Properties tab and change the color next to the color block.

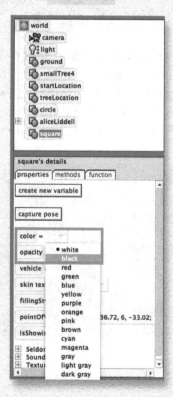

6 **Click the Furniture category. Add 5–10 items to the scene from the Furniture category by clicking and dragging them into your scene. Make sure the items are at the bottom and in front of the square.**

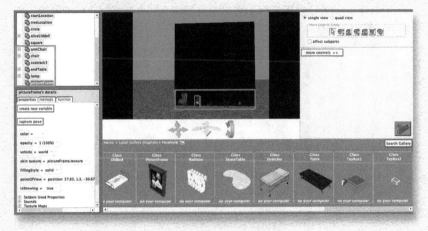

Use the camera controls, as you did in Step 2 in this section, to put some space between the camera and the black square that you added in Step 3. Add objects from the Furniture category by dragging the objects in front of the square. Use the object movement buttons to move the objects in a line in front of the square, on the ground. After you have all your objects in a line, move the camera closer to the square again so that the entire square is covering the screen again. You may not be able to see the furniture anymore, which is okay! Soon you will use code to make the furniture move up, and you will see it.

7   Add an invisible sphere to the camera's location and set
    its point of view to the camera also, just as you did in
    Steps 1–8 in the section called "Set Up Your Camera" in
    Project 2. Rename the sphere **scene1to2Location**.
    The next four images show you each part of completing
    this step.

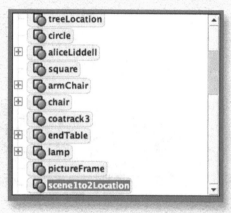

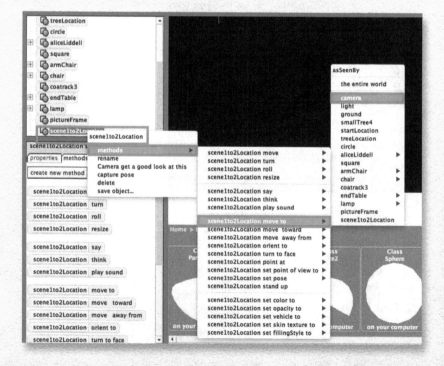

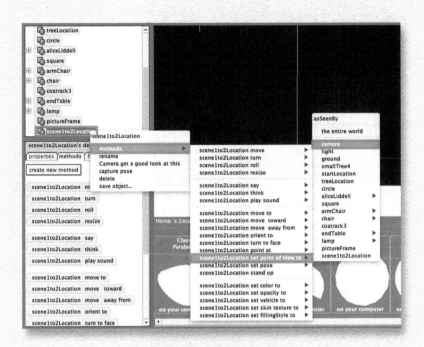

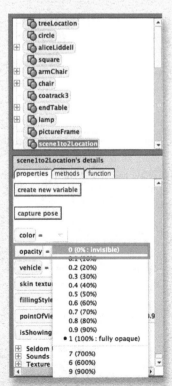

8 For each object that you added in front of the black square, make it invisible by clicking the object in the Object Tree, clicking Properties, and changing the opacity to 0%, just as you did for the sphere in Step 7.

CODE THE SCENE TRANSITION

Now that the scene transition between Scene 1 (the tree) and Scene 2 (the tea party) is set up, it's time to code it!

1 Click the World in the Object Tree and click **create new method** under the methods tab.

2 Name the method **scene1to2**.

3 Drag two **Do together** tiles into the new **scene1to2** method.

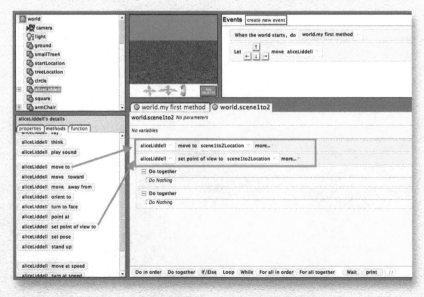

4 Click aliceLidell on the Object pane and drag a **move to** and **set point of view to** block before the first **Do together**. Choose the **scene1to2Location** as the object that she should move to and set point of view to.

5 For each item that should float up in front of the square, drag a **set opacity to** ⇨ **100%**, which you find under the Properties tab for each object. Add these blocks to the second Do together. These blocks should be inside the first Do together block.

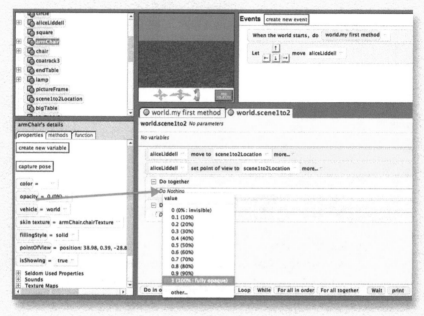

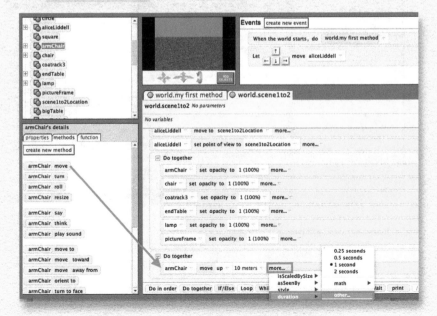

6 For each item that should float up in front of the square, drag a move ⇨ up ⇨ 10 meters into the second Do together block. Then, under more, change the duration to 7–10 seconds.

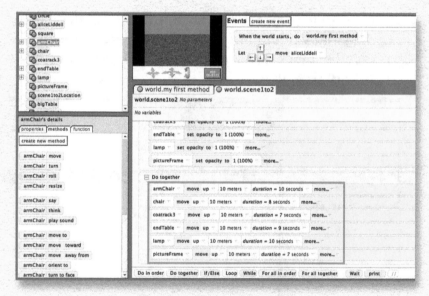

7 Click aliceLidell in the Object Tree, and on the Function tab of aliceLidell's details, click **create new function**.

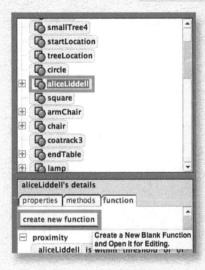

8 Name the function **touchedHole** and change the type to Boolean.

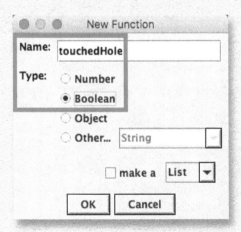

9 Drag an **If/Else** statement into the **touchedHole** function and choose **true**.

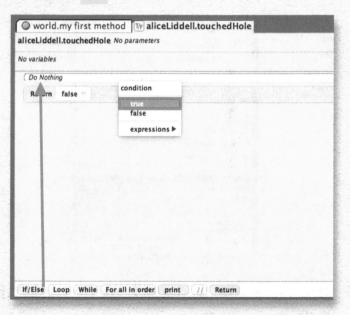

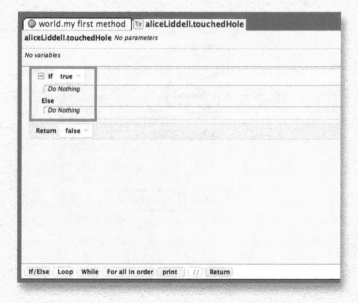

10 On the Function tab of aliceLidell's details, drag an **is within threshold of object** code block into the If statement and choose **1 meter** and **circle**.

11 Drag a **Return** into the If statement and change the **<None>** to true. Then, make sure that the final Return (the final line in the following figure) shows false.

This means that the function will be true if Alice is within 1 meter of the circle, and false if she is farther away.

12 Add a new event called **While something is true.**

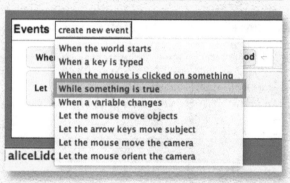

13 Right-click the new event and change it to **When something becomes true.**

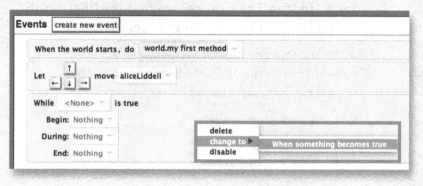

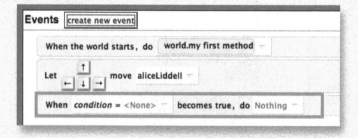

14 **Change the condition to call the touchedHole function. To do this, click condition=<None> and find touchedHole in the pop-up menu under expressions.**

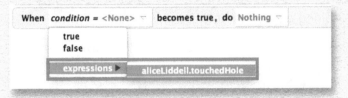

15 **Change the do Nothing to do scene1to2.**

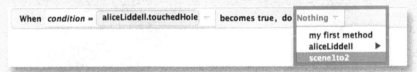

Now your event should call scene1to2 when Alice gets within 1 meter of the circle!

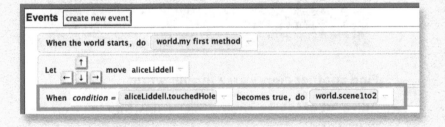

When you go to test this part, you might find that the furniture objects appear and start floating up right when you start the game. This might be because Alice is already too close to the circle. You can move Alice a little farther from the circle. Click Add Objects and then use the object movement buttons to move her. Or, you can change it in the code in Step 10 from 1 meter to something smaller, like 0.5 meters. That will put Alice closer to the circle to make the furniture objects appear and move up.

PREPARE SCENE 2

Finally, you can create Scene 2! This section doesn't walk you through everything because the instructions are very similar to the falling-down-the-hole scene and Scene 1 from Project 2.

The scene you will make should look like this:

1 Find another empty area in your world.

2 Add a lot of tables, chairs, tea kettles, and tea cups to your world.

3 Add a Hare, Mouse, and Mad Hatter (this book uses the Duck Prince) to the tables.

4 Make all the new objects and characters invisible.

5 Add another invisible sphere named teaPartyLocation. Move the sphere to the camera and set its point of view to the camera.

CODE SCENE 2

When your scene is set up, you can code it by following these steps:

1 **Create a new method for the world called scene2.**

2 **Add a Do together and set all the new objects and characters that you added for Scene 2 to 100% opacity.**

Do just as you did in Step 5 of the section "Code the Scene Transition," earlier in this project.

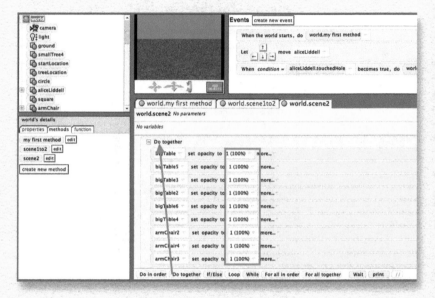

3 Add a Loop 2 times underneath the Do together and put two Do togethers inside the loop. Then have the three characters (in this case, the hare, the mouse, and the duck prince) say, "A very merry unbirthday to you!"

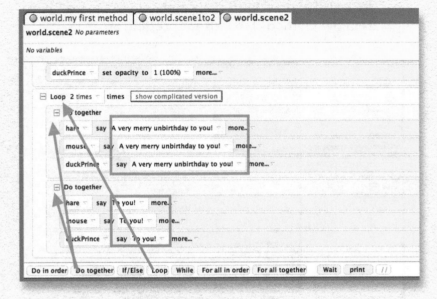

4 Go back to your scene1to2 method and add these blocks of code: move to to move Alice to the teaPartyLocation; and set point of view to to set Alice's point of view to the teaPartyLocation. Then call scene2. To call scene2, click the world in the Object pane and drag the scene2 block from the Methods tab into your coding area.

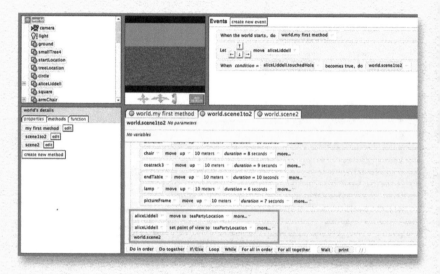

Make sure you're testing as you go! Everything you add should make the game more enjoyable, not break your code. If you get stuck, don't worry! Just head to https://www.thewecan.zone/designing-3d-digital-games to find a set of videos that can walk you through some of the tricky parts. You'll also find a forum there in which you can ask your questions.

CODE THE ENDING

You're almost there! All you have to do is make the ending. At the tea party, players should click around. If they click the correct object, they get a cake. Otherwise, Alice hears the Queen yell, "OFF WITH HER HEAD!" In this version of the game, the Queen won't actually be in the game, so you will have the camera yell those words and pretend that the Queen is somewhere in her castle where we can't see her, yelling *very* loudly.

1 **Create a new method called ending.**

2 **Add a new event called When the mouse is clicked on something.**

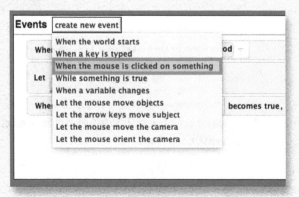

3 Change the Do Nothing to do ending.

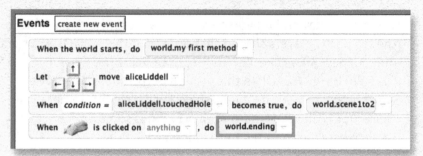

4 Click create new parameter to add a parameter to the ending method called clickedOn that is of type Object.

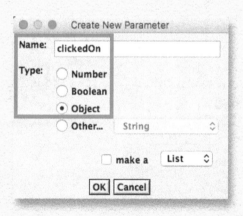

5 Change the event to have clickedOn be expression ⇨ object under mouse cursor.

The world.ending from Step 3 now has ClickedOn = click on the ClickedOn = and click object under mouse cursor under expressions in the pop-up menu.

Events | create new event

When the world starts, do | world.my first method –

Let ↑ ← ↓ → | move aliceLiddell –

When *condition* = | aliceLiddell.touchedHole – | becomes tr[ue]

When 🧽 is clicked on anything – , do | world.ending

| armChair |
| camera |
| light |
| ground |
| smallTree4 |
| startLocation |
| treeLocation |
| circle |
| aliceLiddell ▶ |
| square |
| armChair ▶ |
| chair ▶ |
| coatrack3 |
| endTable ▶ |
| lamp ▶ |
| pictureFrame |
| scene1to2Location |
| bigTable |
| bigTable5 |
| bigTable3 |
| bigTable2 |
| bigTable6 |
| bigTable4 |
| armChair2 ▶ |
| armChair4 ▶ |
| armChair3 ▶ |
| chair2 ▶ |
| chair3 ▶ |
| kidsChair ▶ |
| kidsChair2 ▶ |
| mug ▶ |
| mug2 ▶ |
| teapot ▶ |
| teapot2 ▶ |
| teapot3 ▶ |
| hare ▶ |
| mouse ▶ |
| duckPrince ▶ |
| teaPartyLocation |

world.scene1to2 | ○ world.scene2 | ○ world.ending

create new param

create new varia[ble]

Loop | While | For all in order | For all together | Wait | prin[t]

expressions ▶ | object under mouse cursor

Events | create new event

When the world starts, do | world.my first method –

Let ↑ ← ↓ → | move aliceLiddell –

When *condition* = | aliceLiddell.touchedHole – | becomes true, do | world.scene1to2 –

When 🧽 is clicked on anything – , do | world.ending *clickedOn* = | object under mouse cursor more... | – | –

6 Drag an If statement into the ending method.

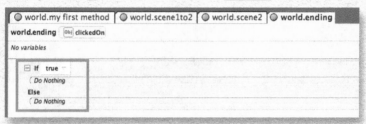

7 Drag the clickedOn parameter into the True of the If statement. Choose == and then choose the object that you want to be your special winning object.

8 Drag the say code block to inside the **If** part of your **If** statement and choose Other for the phrase. When the pop-up text box appears in the center of your screen, have the duckPrince invite Alice to join the party.

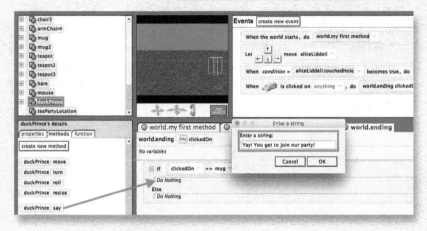

9 In the Else part of the If statement, have the **camera say** "OFF WITH HER HEAD!"

This is the same as Step 8, but you're making the camera instead of the duckPrince say something. Remember, because the Queen isn't actually in your game, you are pretending that the Queen is somewhere you can't see her, so we just have the camera say the phrase and pretend it's the Queen saying it.

This happens if a player clicks an incorrect object.

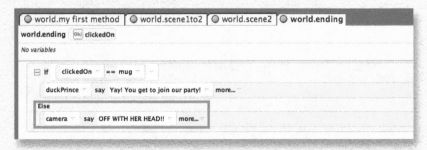

Make sure that you test your code. When you get to the end, don't forget to click your objects to get the final messages that you just included in Steps 8 and 9.

Wow! You've done incredible work. Creating a video game is *really* hard work. But don't worry: If you get stuck, you can always visit the website where I post videos about these and other Alice projects and have a forum where you can ask questions. Just go to https://www.thewecan.zone/designing-3d-digital-games and check it out!

PROJECT 4 CREATE AN ESCAPE ROOM MAZE

YOU'VE MADE IT TO THE FINAL PROJECT! A lot of this project will use what you learned in the previous three projects, so if you get stuck, just revisit the first part of this book. In this project, you are going to create a maze of buildings and rooms. You will add fun controls that will move players all around the world. You will even add non-player characters (Artificial Intelligence) to interact with the players!

DESIGN YOUR ESCAPE ROOM MAZE

This part will take some creativity on your part. This section will walk you through how to make the first room, but then you can add many more rooms on your own.

While you are designing your escape room maze, you will have to use the camera controls at the bottom of the scene.

1 Click Add Objects to set up your scene.

2 Under the Buildings category, add a factory to your world.

3 Under the Environments category, add a Class Bedroom to your world, behind the factory so that you can't see it.

4 Move the camera to the bedroom door. Add a sphere to the world, move it to the camera, set its points of view to be the camera, and make it invisible. Rename the sphere **FirstRoom**.

5 From the Controls category, add a switch to the fireplace in the room. Make the switch larger and use the object controls to move it to the right position.

6 From the Environments category, add a Corridor1 right behind the fireplace.

7 Move the camera to the entryway of the corridor, just behind the fireplace, and add a second sphere. Move the sphere to the camera, set its point of view to the camera, and make it invisible. Then name the sphere FirstCorridor.

8 **From the Environments category, add a hedgemaze to the end of your corridor. You might want to make the hedgemaze bigger so that your players can't see over it.**

If you have to move your camera up in the sky to get a good look at your scene, you can always right-click the camera in the Object pane and use move to and set point of view to with one of your previous sphere locations, like FirstCorridor.

9 Move the camera through the door and into the hedgemaze. Then add another invisible sphere to your camera's location and point of view and name it Maze.

10 From the Environments category, add an **EndRoom** to the exit of your maze. Make it larger so that you can fit more enemies inside (coming later in the project).

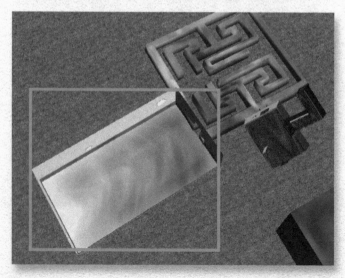

11 Move the camera to the entrance of the EndRoom and add an invisible sphere named End to its location and point of view.

12 Move the camera in front of the factory, add a sphere to the world, move the sphere to the camera, and set its point of view to the camera. Then make the sphere invisible and From the Controls category, add a button to the door of the factory and make it large. The button looks like a red cylinder on a silver square.

Your entire scene should look something like the following image.

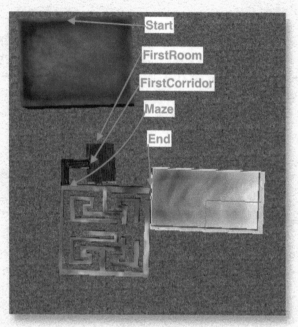

CODE YOUR CONTROLS

Great job — now you have an escape room maze! It's time to add some code so that your players can move the camera around like a character and interact with the switches and buttons that you put around the maze.

A lot of the Alice environments let players just walk right through the walls. This is a feature of Alice that is not easily fixed. So when your players play the game, you have to encourage them to stay within the walls and not cheat!

SET UP YOUR CONTROLS

1 Add a new event called **Let the arrow keys move subject.**

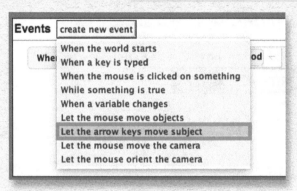

2 Make sure the subject is the **camera.**

3 Add three new events called **When the mouse is clicked on something.**

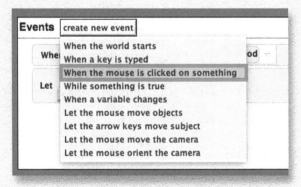

4 Have the objects that the mouse clicks be the switch, the button, and the corridor door's inside doorknob.

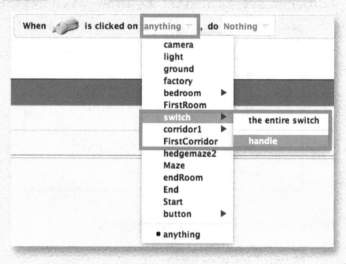

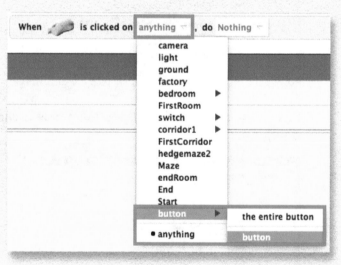

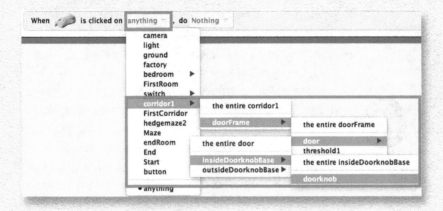

5 Create three new methods called EnterTheMaze, WalkThroughTheFireplace, and EnterTheRoom.

When naming objects and methods, it is always best to make the names readable. Spell the words correctly and use full words, not just letters. You can also use capital letters to make the names more readable. For example, EnterTheMaze is a good name for a method because it is easy to read each word, plus the name describes what is going to happen in that method (the player will enter the maze). If instead you just called this method Enter, you might not remember whether it's having the player enter the room, the hallway, or the maze! You can also make the first word lowercase, as in enterTheMaze, which is still readable.

6 Change the Nothing in the three events from Step 3 to be WalkThroughTheFireplace for the switch, EnterTheRoom for the button, and EnterTheMaze for the doorknob.

DEFINE YOUR CONTROLS

Now that you have all your controls set up, you can actually make the camera move to the correct locations when the controls are activated.

1 In your EnterTheRoom method, add a Do together with a move to and a set point of view to to the code block inside it:

» **move to:** Drag a camera move to block and choose FirstRoom from the pop-up menu. Then click more and choose *duration* = 0.25 seconds from the pop-up menu. Click more again and choose *style* = abruptly.

» **set point of view to:** Set the point of view of the camera to the FirstRoom sphere. Click more to change the *duration* = 0.25 seconds and *style* = abruptly, as you did for the move to.

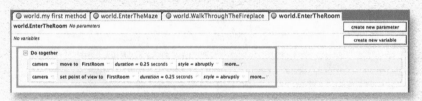

2 **In your WalkThroughTheFireplace method, perform the exact same actions as you did in Step 1 for the EnterTheRoom method, except move and set the point of view of the camera to the FirstCorridor sphere instead of FirstRoom.**

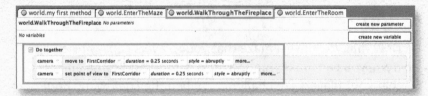

3 **In your EnterTheMaze method, perform the exact same actions as you did in Steps 1 and 2, except move and set the point of view of the camera to the Maze sphere instead.**

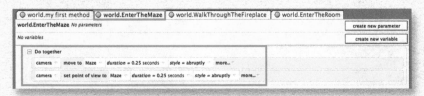

The order of the tabs of your methods doesn't matter when they are opened in your coding area. As you may have noticed, in Steps 1–3 of this section, you coded the EnterTheRoom method first, even though it is the far-right tab. EnterTheRoom was the first method because it makes more logical sense. The player will first enter the room, then walk through the fireplace, then enter the maze. If you close the method tab by right-clicking and choosing Close, and then you re-open the method by clicking Edit, the order of the tabs will change. So remember: The order of tabs doesn't matter, but the order of your coding blocks does!

Test your game! To do that, click Play and make sure that all your controls work. If your sphere locations are wrong, go back to editing the scene by clicking Add Objects underneath the scene above the coding area. Then you can change your sphere locations.

ADD ENEMIES TO YOUR MAZE

Now that you have a maze that your players can try to escape from, you can make things a little harder! Add some enemies so that your players are challenged when they get to the EndRoom.

1 From the Spooky category, add **five zombies** to the EndRoom.

2 Add a **sphere** to the world, make it smaller, and rename it SnowBall. Snowballs are a great defense against zombies!

To change the size of an object, find the buttons next to the scene editor (after you have clicked Add Objects) and use the second-to-last button with four arrows coming out of the face. To rename an object, right-click the object you want to rename in the Object Tree pane and choose Rename.

3 **From the Special Effects category, add some smoke and fire to the EndRoom for dramatic effect.**

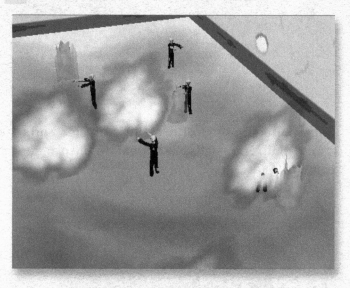

MAKE YOUR ENEMIES MOVE AROUND

Now that your enemies are in place, it's time to add some Artificial Intelligence (AI) to make them move around on their own.

1 Add a new event called While something is true. Right-click it and change it to When something becomes true.

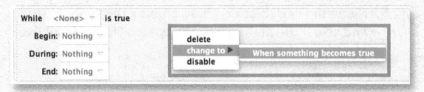

2 Change the condition to camera is within 1 meter of End.

This will make the event call the method when the camera gets to the End sphere location.

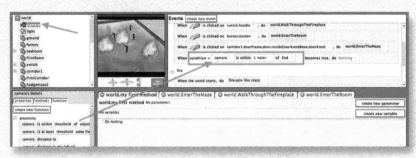

3 Make a new method called Attack and change Nothing in the event to Attack.

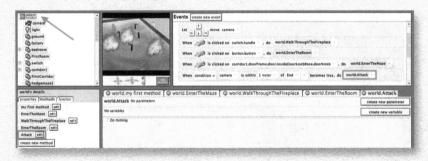

4   Click world in the Object pane and go to the Properties
    tab. Choose create new variable.

5   Name the variables zombies, change the Type to Object,
    and select the make a Box to say List. Then add all five
    zombies as items in the list.

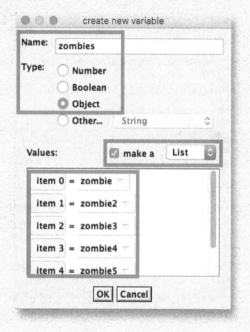

*The neat thing about coding is that you can have
one variable represent more than one object.
Sometimes you have a variable that represents one
object, like one zombie. But in Alice, you can also
have a variable represent a list of objects. In Step 5,
the variable called zombies represents all your
zombies. This lets you tell every zombie in the list to
do something instead of telling each zombie one at a
time. You will do this in Step 6.*

6 In your Attack method, drag a **For all together block** and choose **world.zombies** from the expressions pop-up menu.

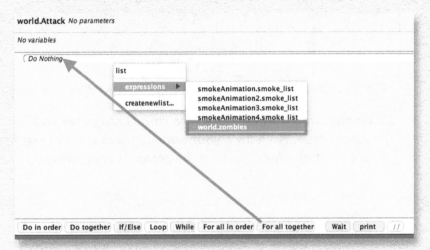

7 Drag the **item_from_zombies** block into the **For all together** and choose **move forward 0.5 meters.**

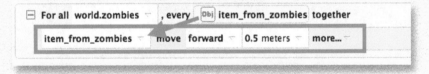

8 Click the world in the Object pane and then click the Function tab. Drag a **random number** block into the 0.5 meters of the item_from_zombie move forward code block. Change the minimum to 0.25 and the maximum to 2.

9 Repeat Steps 7 and 8, but this time choose turn left as the method, 0.25 as the minimum, and 0.75 as the maximum.

10 Finally, drag a While block into your coding area and choose true. Then drag your For all together block inside of your While block so that the zombies keep moving!

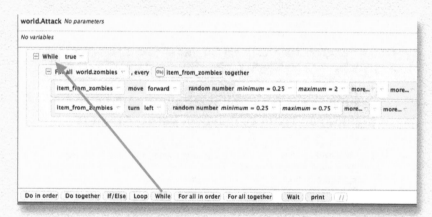

Now you should test the game to make sure the zombies are moving around randomly.

Don't forget to move your camera back to the start, right in front of the first room. You can also add a few lines of code to your world.my first method to make sure that the camera always starts in the correct location. For example, add a Start sphere to the front of the room, just as you have done for all your other location spheres in this project. Then you can add a move to and set point of view to code block to world.my first method so that when the world starts, the camera goes to the start location every time.

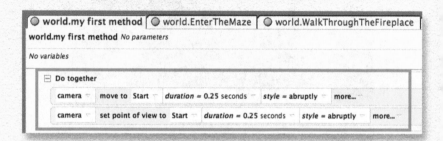

MAKE YOUR ENEMIES TRY TO DEFEAT YOUR PLAYERS

The final part of this project is to make sure that your players can defeat the enemies (zombies), or have the zombies defeat the players!

1 Under the Properties tab for world, click create new variable. In the pop-up window, name the variable health, set Type as Number, and set Value as 10. Then click OK.

2 Change the While loop in your Attack method to be While health > 0. To do this, click the Properties tab for world and drag the health variable you just created over the true part of your While loop. A pop-up menu will appear that will let you choose Health >, and then you can follow the menu to pick 0.

This will make the zombies keep attacking until the player's health runs out.

3 Drag an If statement into the For all together.

4 Click any of the zombies in your Object pane. Click the Function tab for the zombie and drag a zombie is within threshold of object code block from the Functions pane. A pop-up menu will appear. Choose 1 meter for the threshold and camera for the object.

5 Drag the item_from_zombies and replace the zombie in the zombie is within 1 meter of camera from Step 4 with the item_from_zombies.

6 Click the world in the Object pane. Then click the Properties tab. Drag the **health** variable from the Properties tab into the If statement. In the pop-up menu that appears, choose **decrement world.health by 1.**

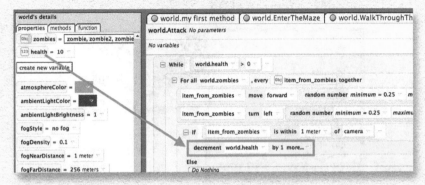

7 Add a Do together into your If statement. Move the decrement world.Health by 1 block into the Do together. Add a camera say "Ow!" code block inside the Do together so that the camera (which is representing the player) says "Ow!" at the same time that the health variable is being decremented by 1.

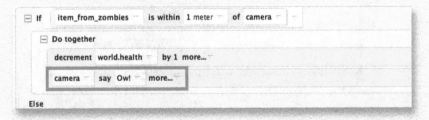

8 Click the light in the Object pane and then click the
Properties tab for the light. Drag the color block for the
light outside the While loop. When the pop-up menu
appears, choose black for the color. This will change the
color of the light to black.

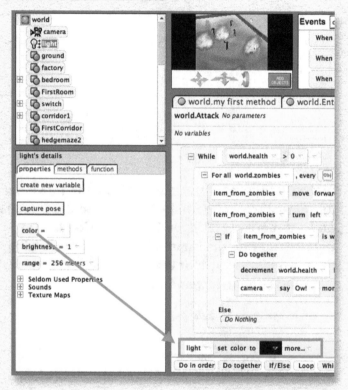

9 Add a few lines of code to do the following: Let players know that their health is gone; make the light white again; set the players' health back to 10; and then have them start over from the beginning.

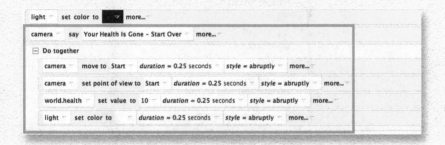

Great job! Now you have the zombies attacking your players! ! In the next section, you will set the code so that your players can actually win!

Test your code to make sure that if a zombie hits you ten times, you start all over again.

CREATE CODE FOR WINNING THE GAME

In this section, your players get to throw snowballs at the zombies to defeat them before they defeat the players.

1 Create a new **method** called **Defend**.

2 Add a new **When the mouse is clicked on something** event and leave the object as anything, but change the method to **Defend**.

3 **Add a parameter to the method Defend called objectClicked that is of type Object.**

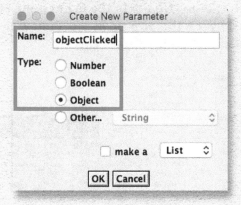

4 Change the parameter at the event to be the object under mouse cursor. To do this, click ObjectClicked=<None> in the Event pane and find **expressions** on the pop-up menu. Follow the menu and choose **object under mouse cursor**.

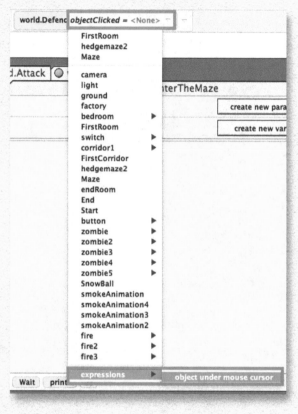

5 Drag an **If** statement to your Defend method and change True to objectClicked == Zombie by dragging the ObjectClicked parameter onto the True. When the pop-up appears, choose objectClicked == and then choose Zombie from the menu.

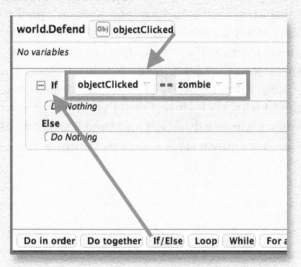

6 Click the down arrow to the right of the If statement and, from the pop-up menu, choose Logic ⇨ either objectClicked == zombie or ⇨ true. Drag objectClicked into the true, and from the pop-up menu, choose objectClicked == zombie2. Do this again for zombie3, zombie4, and zombie5. This will check to see whether any of the five zombies were clicked.

This is a tricky step. You can watch a short video on how to do it if you go to https://www.thewecan. zone/designing-3d-digital-games. Click the screen to stop and start the video if you need to.

7 **Add code to abruptly move the SnowBall to the camera, face the zombie the player clicked on, and become visible, all in 0 seconds. To do this, drag a Do together into the If statement. Then, click the SnowBall in the Object pane and drag three code blocks into the Do Together: move to, turn to face, and set opacity to. When you drag each code block into the Do together, a pop-up menu will appear. Choose camera for move to, expressions ⇨ objectClicked for turn to face, and 1(100%) for set opacity to. Then, for each of the three code blocks, click More. From the pop-up menu that appears, choose duration and then 0 seconds. Do this again but choose style and then abruptly.**

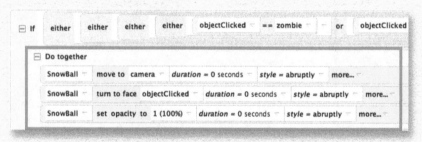

8 **Add code to move the SnowBall forward and then make it disappear by setting the SnowBall's opacity to 0.**

Because you added a code block in Step 3 that had the SnowBall turn to face the object that the player clicked (probably a zombie), the SnowBall will now move toward the zombie to try to hit him!

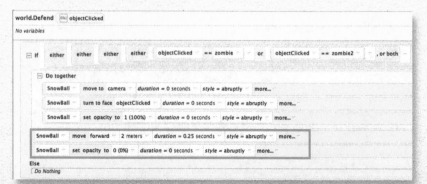

9 Add a new event, While something is true, and right-click to change it to When something becomes true. This is the exact same thing you did in Step 13 of Project 3 in the section "Code the Scene Transition."

10 Add code to the event to check whether the SnowBall is within 0.25 meters of the zombie *and* the SnowBall's Opacity is 1. Then change the <Nothing> to set the zombie's opacity to 0. This event makes the zombie disappear.

This means that if the SnowBall hits the zombie and is visible, the zombie should be defeated.

11 Add this event four more times and change the condition and the event for each of the other zombies.

12 In your Attack method, click the arrow to the right of your If statement. From the pop-up menu, hover on logic and choose item_from_zombies is within 1 meter of camera and. Then choose true from the last pop-up menu that appears.

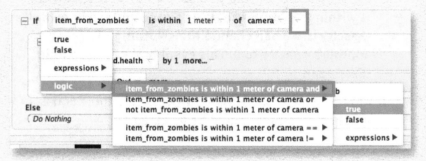

13 Replace the True with zombie opacity == 1.

14 Replace the zombie with item_from_zombies.

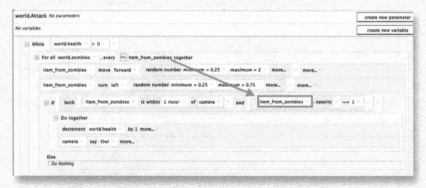

Now each zombie will disappear when the player throws a snowball at it!

15 Create a new variable called **zombiesDefeated** that is a Number with value 0.

16 Create a new method called **CheckIfWon** with a parameter called **zombieHit** that is an Object.

Create New Parameter

Name: zombieHit

Type:
- ○ Number
- ○ Boolean
- ● Object
- ○ Other... String

☐ make a List

OK Cancel

17 Change the five events for when the **SnowBall** is near
each zombie to call the **CheckIfWon** method with each
zombie as the parameter.

18 Add two lines of code to the **CheckIfWon** method to make the zombie invisible and increment the **ZombiesDefeated** variable by 1.

world.CheckIfWon [Obj] zombieHit

No variables

> zombieHit ⌄ set opacity to 0 (0%) ⌄ more... ⌄
>
> increment world.zombiesDefeated ⌄ by 1 more... ⌄

19 Add an **If** statement in your **CheckIfWon** method to check whether all zombies have been defeated. If they have, make all the smoke and fire invisible, make the **EndRoom** invisible, and tell the player "**You Won!!!**"

To make things a little smoother, you can try making the distance between the SnowBall and the zombies bigger, such as 3 meters instead of 1. You can also make your end location sphere larger.

Make sure you test your code in every way you can think of. Making video games is tedious and sometimes tricky, but if you keep at it, you can make anything! You can check out the Escape Room at https://youtu.be/cVMrIhs9IAM. Notice that everything isn't perfect, and that is okay!

ABOUT THE AUTHOR

Sarah Guthals received her PhD from University of California, San Diego, in Computer Science specializing in CS Education in 2014. During graduate school, she built the beta version of CodeSpells, a 3D immersive video game designed to teach children to code through playing a wizard and writing "spells." She went on to co-found ThoughtSTEM, a company that builds software (such as LearnToMod), curriculum, and pedagogies for teaching children to code and empowering K-12 teachers to teach their students. She has written four books around Minecraft and one on mobile development, launched a Coursera and EdX course for teachers interested in teaching coding, and was recently named Forbes 30 under 30 in Science. She founded We Can, a company dedicated to encouraging *all* kids to do anything. Her passion is making coding accessible to everyone, with the goal of making it a basic literacy.

DEDICATION

I would like to dedicate this book to my close friends and family members who have supported me, not only in writing this book but also in becoming who I am today. I specifically dedicate this book to Adrian Guthals, who has always helped me to see that, with passion and dedication, I can really do anything I want.

AUTHOR'S ACKNOWLEDGMENTS

I want to acknowledge all of the hard work that went into making Alice. Without these amazing engineers, making 3D video games would be so much harder. I also acknowledge the teachers and parents around the world who have recognized the importance of coding in teaching so many valuable lessons to our next generation of makers. Finally, a huge acknowledgement to Susan Christophersen, the editor, and Drake Kegley, the technical editor. Drake's dedication to working through all the projects ensured that kids using this book can learn to code even easier!

PUBLISHER'S ACKNOWLEDGMENTS

Acquisitions Editor: Amy Fandrei

Project and Copy Editor: Susan Christophersen

Technical Editor: Drake Kegley

Sr. Editorial Assistant: Cherie Case

Production Editor: Vasanth Koilraj

CPSIA information can be obtained
at www.ICGtesting.com
Printed in the USA
BVHW052051210821
614355BV00003B/20